Problem Solving

Written by Christine Hood

Illustrations by Viviana Garofoli

FlashKids

An imprint of Sterling Children's Books

This book belongs to

_____

FLASH KIDS, STERLING, and the distinctive Sterling logo are registered trademarks of
Sterling Publishing Co., Inc.

Published by Sterling Publishing Co., Inc.
387 Park Avenue South, New York, NY 10016
Text and illustrations © 2007 by Flash Kids
Distributed in Canada by Sterling Publishing
c/o Canadian Manda Group, 165 Dufferin Street
Toronto, Ontario, Canada M6K 3H6
Distributed in the United Kingdom by GMC Distribution Services
Castle Place, 166 High Street, Lewes, East Sussex, England BN7 1XU
Distributed in Australia by Capricorn Link (Australia) Pty. Ltd.
P.O. Box 704, Windsor, NSW 2756, Australia

Sterling ISBN 978-1-4114-6298-4

Printed in Canada

Lot #:
3 5 7 9 10 8 6 4 2
05/12

For information about custom editions, special sales, premium and
corporate purchases, please contact Sterling Special Sales
Department at 800-805-5489 or specialsales@sterlingpublishing.com.

Cover design and production by Mada Design, Inc.

Dear Parent,

Learning to solve problems is one of the most important skills in math. *Problem Solving* will help your child to look at problems with a critical eye. This book includes fun activities that help your child use logic, estimate, and choose a method to solve a problem. To get the most from *Problem Solving,* follow these simple steps:

- Provide a comfortable and quiet place for your child to work.
- Encourage your child to work at his or her own pace.
- Help your child with the problems if he or she needs it.
- Offer lots of praise and support.
- Most of all, remember that learning should be fun!

Visit us at *www.flashkidsbooks.com* for free downloads, informative articles, and valuable parent resources!

Temperatures around the World

Read each problem carefully, then solve it. Show your work.

1. The absolute coldest it can get anywhere is −460°F. This is considered "absolute zero." The coldest air temperatures found on Earth are near the South Pole, which are in the range of −130°F. What is the difference in temperature between the South Pole and absolute zero?

   _____

2. The hottest temperature ever recorded on Earth was 136°F in the Libyan Desert. The coldest temperature ever recorded on Earth was in Vostok, Antarctica. It dropped to −128.6°F. What is the difference between the hottest and coldest temperatures?

   _____

3. Temperatures can rise and fall very quickly. In Springfield, Missouri, in 1955, the temperature fell from 77°F to 13°F overnight. In Browning, Montana, in 1916, the temperature fell from 44°F to −56°F in 24 hours! How many degrees did the temperature fall in Browning? _____
   In which city was the temperature change largest? _____

4. In 1924, the temperature in Fairfield, Montana, was 63°F. It dropped 84°F by midnight. How cold was it at midnight? _____

Dog Days

Read the table. Then answer the questions.

Dog	Height	Weight
German shepherd	2 feet	65.2 pounds
Toy poodle	$\frac{3}{5}$ foot	3.5 pounds
Husky	$3\frac{2}{3}$ feet	83.6 pounds
Beagle	$1\frac{1}{3}$ feet	47.3 pounds
Pug	$1\frac{1}{4}$ feet	32.9 pounds
Dachshund	$\frac{3}{4}$ foot	25.4 pounds

1. What is the difference in weight between the husky and the dachshund?

_____

2. What is the combined height of the pug, German shepherd, and beagle?

_____

3. How much taller is the husky than the toy poodle?

_____

4. What is the combined weight of the pug, husky, and German shepherd?

_____

5. If the husky grew 6 inches, how tall would it be?

_____

Time for Travel

This map of the United States is divided into four time zones.

Use the map to answer the questions on the next page.

1. Brent is flying from San Francisco, CA to Atlanta, GA. His plane departs at 3:35 PM. The flight lasts 5 hours and 17 minutes.
   What time will it be in Atlanta when Brent's plane arrives? _____

2. Falcon Air has two flights going from St. Louis, MO to New York, NY each day. The first flight departs at 8:48 AM. The second flight departs at 2:05 PM. It takes 3 hours and 22 minutes to get from St. Louis to New York.
   What time does the first flight land in New York (Eastern Time)? _____
   What time does the second flight land in New York (Eastern Time)? _____

3. Tyler flew from Seattle to Minneapolis. He departed Seattle at 11:50 AM. The flight lasted 4 hours and 5 minutes. He had 1 hour and 10 minutes before his next flight. He landed in Pittsburgh 2 hours and 13 minutes later.
   What time did Tyler depart Minneapolis (Central Time)?_____
   What time did Tyler land in Pittsburgh (Eastern Time)? _____

4. Leah and Cherie are flying from Boston, MA, to Denver, CO. They have one stop in Kansas City, where they have to wait 1 hour and 40 minutes before their next flight takes off. The flight from Boston to Kansas City departs at 2:25 PM and takes 3 hours and 37 minutes. The flight from Kansas City to Denver takes 1 hour and 12 minutes.
   What time will they arrive in Kansas City (Central Time)? _____
   What time with they arrive in Denver (Mountain Time)? _____

Order of Operations

Help Justin ski down the hill. Read the clues.

Then solve the problems.

Clues:

- Each problem has two steps.
- Use ( ) as your first step to close off two numbers.
- Use two operation signs (x, −, +, ÷).
- Use one equals sign (=).

Example: 63 _____ 36 _____ 9 _____ 3

Answer: 63 = 36 + (9 x 3)

162 _____ 6 _____ (12 _____ 15)

(30 _____ 2) _____ 12 _____ 48

(156 _____ 12) _____ 70 _____ 83

232 _____ (8 _____ 37) _____ 64

(93 _____ 27) _____ 11 _____ 6

45 _____ (80 _____ 12) _____ 1,005

What's the Probability?

Solve the problems.

1. A bowl contains 12 cherry candies, 16 root beer candies, 10 mint candies, 14 lemon candies, and 17 orange candies. What is the probability of pulling out:

   a. a cherry candy? _____

   b. a root beer or a lemon candy?

   _____

   c. a mint or an orange candy?

   _____

2. Keisha, Shawna, Kyle, Anna, Mia, Gilberto, and Anthony are in a study group together. They are choosing in what order to speak for their science presentation. Each student wrote his or her name on a slip of paper and put it in a hat. What is the probability of pulling out:

   a. a girl's name? _____

   b. a boy's name that begins with "K"?

   _____

   c. a name that begins with "A"?

   _____

3. Jacob's bank contains 12 dimes, 4 one-dollar bills, 7 quarters, 26 pennies, 18 nickels, and 6 five-dollar bills. What is the probability of pulling out:

   a. a dime or a penny? _____

   b. paper money?_____

   c. a coin with a value less than 25¢?

   _____

Buying and Leasing Cars

Use the table to answer the questions.

Car	Sale Price	Leasing Cost (per month)
SUV	$32,699	$405
convertible	$27,995	$260
luxury	$25,779	$249
mid-size	$22,195	$189
compact	$19,870	$175

1. How much would it cost to lease a mid-size car for one year?

   _____

2. China wants to lease a luxury car for eight years. Would it cost more to lease the car or buy it? _____

3. Luke is buying a convertible for his 30th birthday. He added a new CD player for $525, tinted the windows for $255, and then had special upholstery installed for $2,749. What was the final cost of the car?_____

4. Tyra's parents want to lease an SUV for seven years. Would it cost more to lease the SUV or buy it? _____

5. Carla is leasing a compact car for three years while she saves money to buy a convertible. Right now she has $18,604 in the bank. After leasing the car, how much more money will she have to save to buy the convertible? (After three years, the price of the convertible will have increased 5%.) _____

Wheel and Deal

Wheels come in a variety of sizes. For each problem, use the information
to find both the diameter and the circumference of the wheels.
Round answers to the nearest whole number.

1. Maya got a new bike cruiser for her birthday.
   The wheels are bright purple and measure 27 inches tall.
   Diameter = _____
   Circumference = _____

2. Jonah's new black truck is huge! Even the tires are big.
   They are exactly one yardstick high.
   Diameter = _____
   Circumference = _____

3. Deena's new wheelchair has large, sturdy wheels. She chose wheels with multi-
   colored, 12-inch spokes. Her doctor told her the spokes are the same size as the
   radius of the wheels.
   Diameter = _____
   Circumference = _____

4. Miguel bought his hamster a new exercise
   wheel. It's twice as big as his old wheel,
   which was 5.5 inches high.
   Diameter = _____
   Circumference = _____

Tricky Triangles

Read this information about triangles. Then solve the problems.

> Obtuse: One angle measures more than 90 degrees.
>
> Acute: Every angle measures less than 90 degrees.
>
> Right: One angle measures 90 degrees.
>
> Equilateral: All angles measure the same.
>
> All the angles in a triangle add up to 180 degrees.

1. I have a right angle and two other angles that measure the same.
   What do my other two angles measure? _____
   What kind of triangle am I?_____

2. I have an angle that is 18 degrees less than a right angle.
   Another angle is 35 degrees.
   What does my third angle measure? _____
   What kind of triangle am I? _____

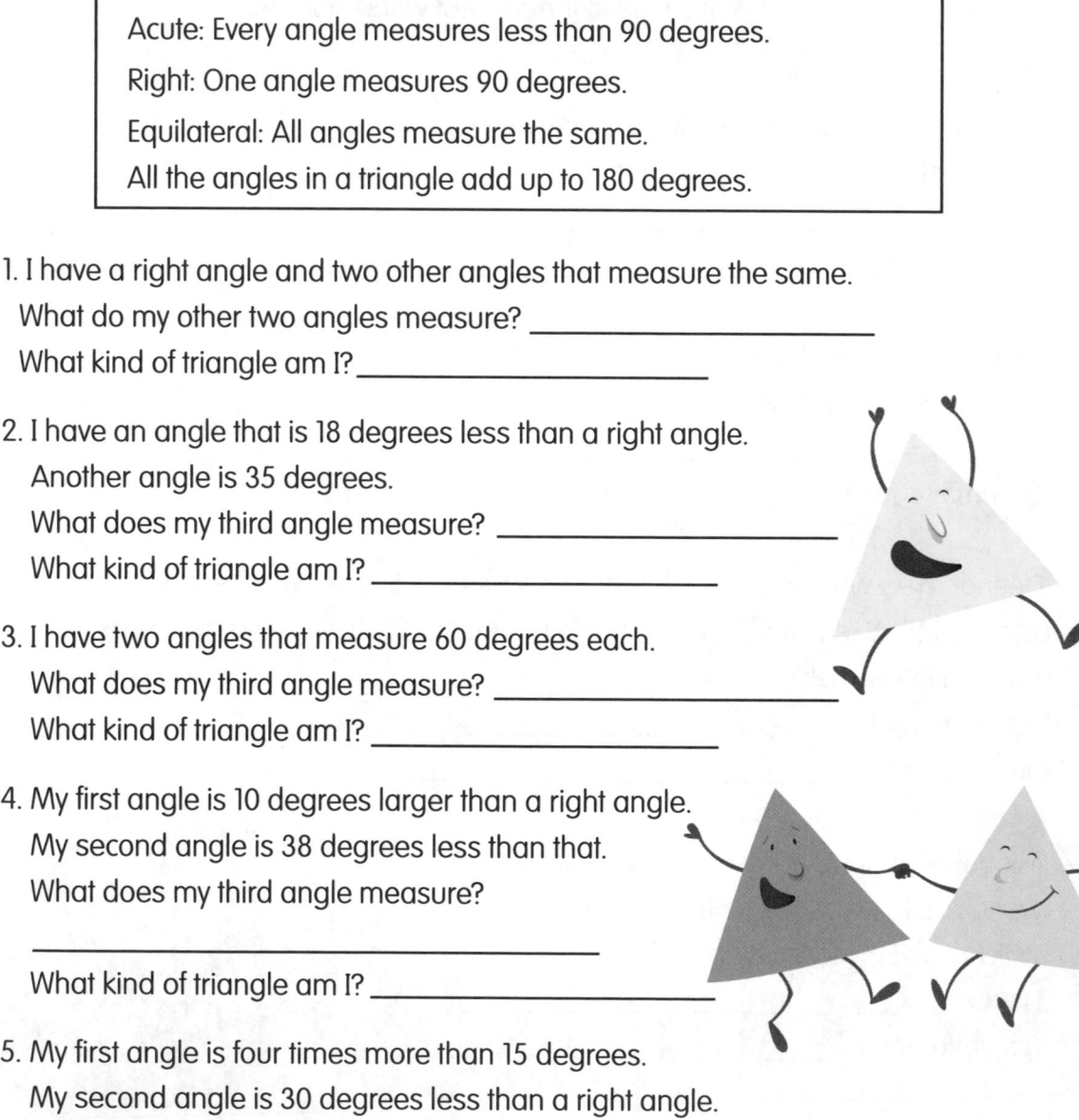

3. I have two angles that measure 60 degrees each.
   What does my third angle measure? _____
   What kind of triangle am I? _____

4. My first angle is 10 degrees larger than a right angle.
   My second angle is 38 degrees less than that.
   What does my third angle measure?

   _____

   What kind of triangle am I? _____

5. My first angle is four times more than 15 degrees.
   My second angle is 30 degrees less than a right angle.
   What does my third angle measure? _____
   What kind of triangle am I?_____

Lunchtime!

It's lunchtime at the Rainforest Café. Read the
menu. Then answer the questions.

Rainforest Café

Sandwiches:

Roast Turkey $3.85

Roast Beef $4.25

Vegetarian $4.50

Salads:

Caesar $5.35

Garden $4.00

Extras:

Cheese $1.00

Chips $0.75

Pasta Salad $1.15

Lunch Special: $5.75

½ Sandwich

Small Salad

Chips

1. Brian spent $6.00 for lunch. What three items did he choose? _____

_____

2. Cassie is taking lunch orders for her friends at work. She bought two lunch
   specials, three Caesar salads, a vegetarian sandwich, and three bags of chips.
   How much money did she spend? _____

3. Kendra and Jon have $15 between them. Kendra got the lunch special. Jon got a
   garden salad, chips, and a side of pasta salad. They left the waiter a 15% tip.

   How much was the tip they left?_____

   How much money did they have leftover? _____

4. Corey spent exactly $11.60 on lunch for him and his brother.

   What five items did they choose? _____

_____

Reading Graphs

Read the graph about California beaches.

Then answer the questions below.

California Beach Attendance, 2006

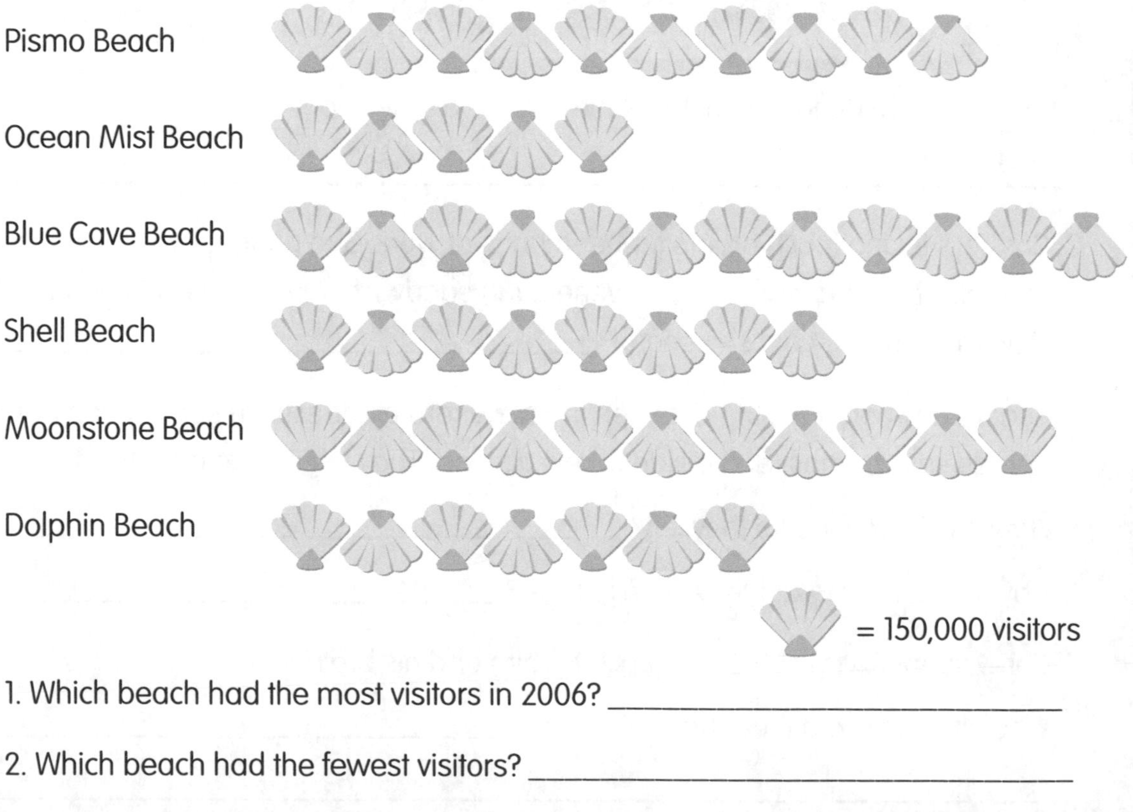

Pismo Beach

Ocean Mist Beach

Blue Cave Beach

Shell Beach

Moonstone Beach

Dolphin Beach

= 150,000 visitors

1. Which beach had the most visitors in 2006? _____

2. Which beach had the fewest visitors? _____

3. Which beach had more visitors, Shell Beach or Dolphin Beach?

_____

4. How many more visitors did Moonstone Beach have than Ocean Mist Beach?

_____

5. How many more visitors would Shell Beach need in order to have the most
   visitors of all the beaches? _____

6. What is the total number of visitors for all the beaches?

_____

7. Write the names of the beaches in order, from least visitors to most visitors. Then
   write how many visitors they had.

_____   _____

_____   _____

_____   _____

_____   _____

_____   _____

_____   _____

Big Budgets

Isel just got her first apartment. It's time to start budgeting!

Her job as a veterinary assistant pays $25,000 per year.

To make sure she has enough money,

Isel has written out her yearly budget in percentages.

1. Write out Isel's budget in dollar amounts:

Rent	20%	_____
Utilities (gas, water, electric)	8%	_____
Clothing	10%	_____
Food	12%	_____
Car	9%	_____
Medical	4%	_____
Taxes	10%	_____
Savings	5%	_____
Entertainment	8%	_____
Miscellaneous	14%	_____

Answer these questions about Isel's budget.
Round up to the next whole number as needed.

2. Isel's monthly rent is $450.
   Has she budgeted enough money for rent?

   _____

   About how much more does she need each month to pay rent?

   _____

3. Isel reduced her clothing budget by 2%.
   How much more money does she have in her budget?

   _____

   Can she afford her rent now? _____

4. Isel sold her car. She put half the money budgeted for car expenses
   in savings and spent the other half on miscellaneous items.
   How much money did she add to savings?

   _____

   How much total money is now set aside for miscellaneous items?

   _____

5. Isel wants to reduce her entertainment budget by 3%. How much money
   will she have left for entertainment?_____

6. Isel needs to add 2.5% to her budget to cover rising utility costs.
   How much less will she have in her budget?

   _____

Pinky's Pizza Parlor

You can choose any two toppings you want at Pinky's Pizza Parlor.
All pizzas come with cheese. The topping choices are: pepperoni, onions, ham, olives, mushrooms, sausage, pineapple, and peppers. List all the possible topping combinations.

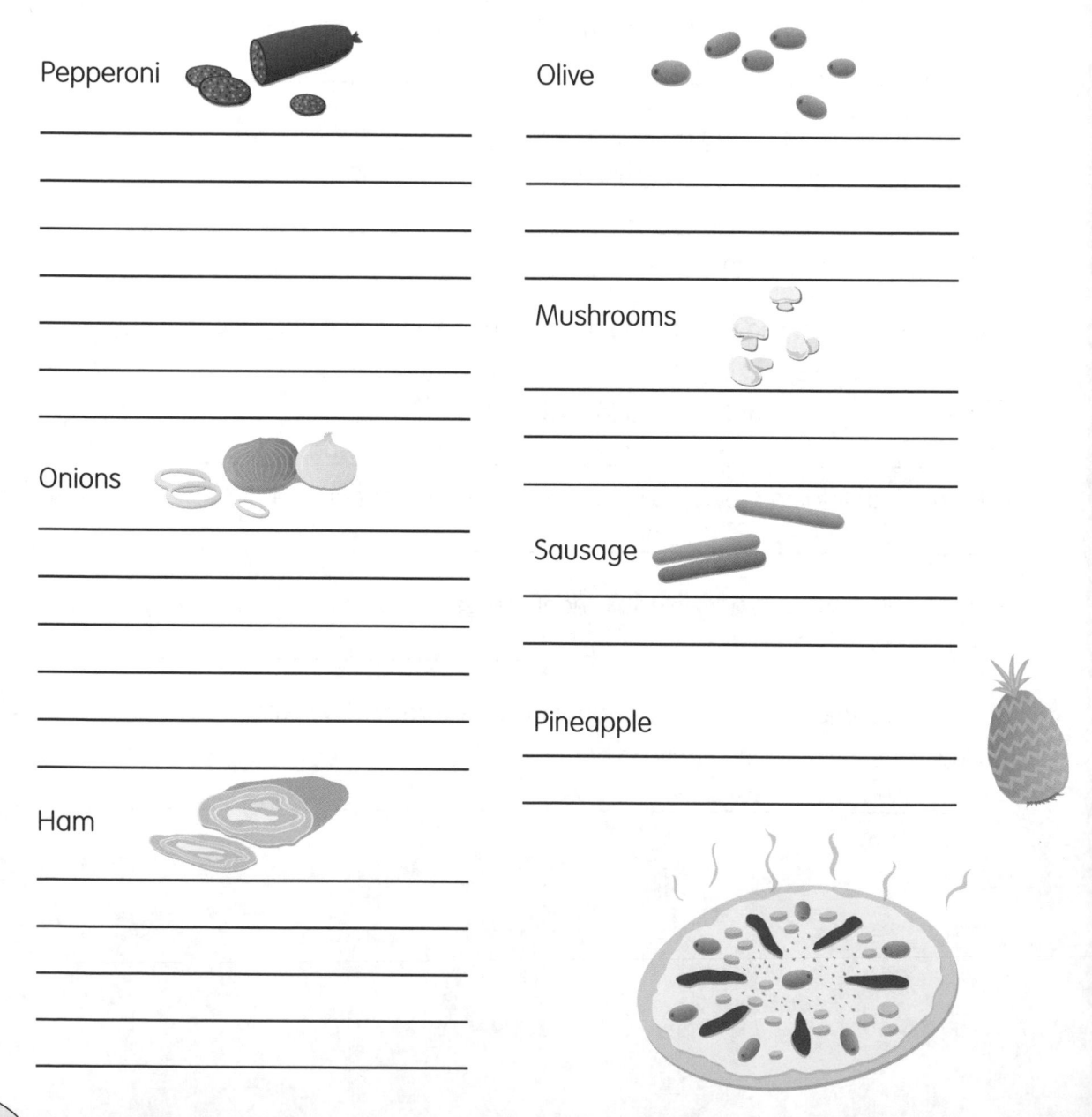

Pepperoni

_____
_____
_____
_____
_____

Onions

_____
_____
_____
_____

Ham

_____
_____
_____
_____

Olive

_____
_____
_____

Mushrooms

_____
_____
_____

Sausage

_____
_____

Pineapple

_____
_____

Good Cooking

Shawna and her friends are making food for the local homeless shelter.
Fill in each recipe card to show how much of each ingredient is needed.

Chocolate Chip Cookies

Ingredient	1 dozen	12 dozen	15 dozen
shortening	1 cup		
sugar	$1\frac{2}{3}$ cups		
eggs	2		
flour	$4\frac{1}{4}$ cups		
vanilla	$1\frac{1}{2}$ tsp.		
baking soda	$\frac{3}{4}$ tsp.		
chocolate chips	$1\frac{1}{3}$ cups		

Spaghetti with Marina Sauce

Ingredient	1 recipe	6 recipes	13 recipes
tomatoes	3 pounds		
chicken stock	$5\frac{1}{2}$ cups		
garlic	4 cloves		
basil	$1\frac{1}{4}$ tsp.		
oregano	2 tsp.		
spaghetti	1 pound		

Finding Volume

Volume is the area that fills a space, such as a cube (box) or a sphere (ball).

To find the volume, multiply the length by the width by the height.

Volume is recorded in cubic units.

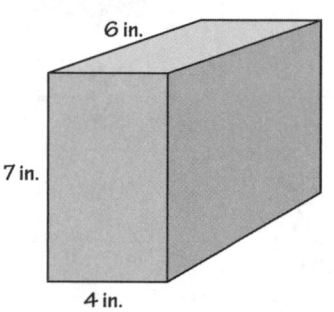

Formula: V = length x width x height

V = 6 in. x 4 in. x 7 in. = 168 cubic inches

1. Kristin's dad is building a pool in the backyard. The pool will be 25 feet wide, 40 feet long, and 6 feet deep.

   How many cubic feet of water will the pool hold? _____

2. Darius is packing old clothes in boxes to donate to the Red Cross. Box A is 3 feet high, 2 feet long, and 3 feet wide. Box B is 3 feet long, 4 feet high, and 1 foot wide.

   Which box holds more clothes? _____

   How many more cubic feet of clothes does it hold? _____

3. Mr. Granger's sixth grade class is building an aquarium. The aquarium will be $4\frac{1}{2}$ feet long, 2 feet wide, and $3\frac{1}{3}$ feet high.

   How many cubic feet of water will the aquarium hold? _____

4. To fill the bottom of the aquarium in question 3, the class needs gravel. The gravel should be 6 inches deep.

   How many cubic inches of gravel will they need? _____

   If a bag of gravel holds 30 cubic inches, how many bags will they need? _____

Ice Cream Survey

Justin is doing a school survey. He wants to find out students' favorite ice cream flavors. He put his results in a circle graph. Read the circle graph and answer the questions. Round up to the next whole number if needed.

Favorite Ice Cream Flavors

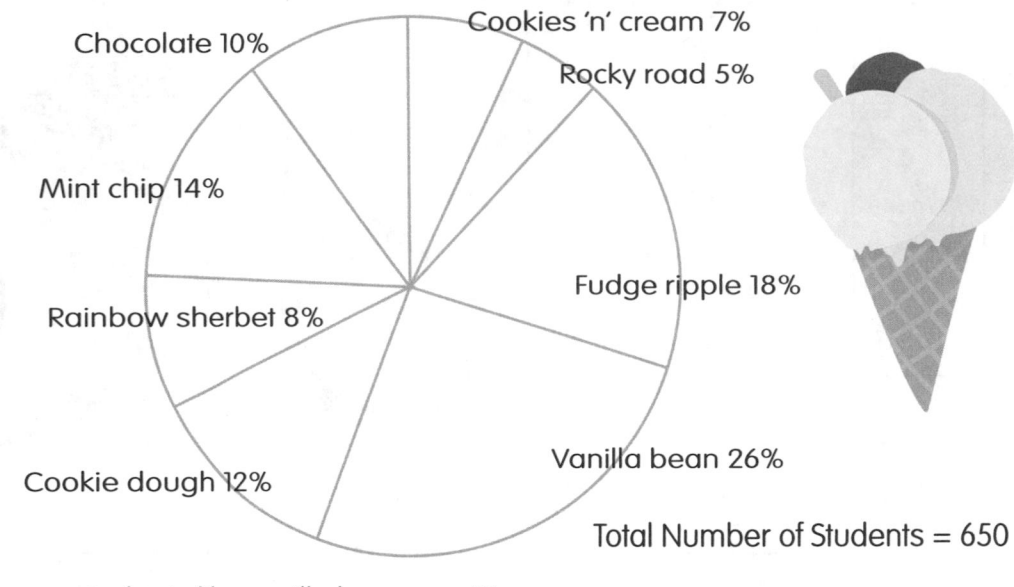

Cookies 'n' cream 7%
Rocky road 5%
Chocolate 10%
Mint chip 14%
Fudge ripple 18%
Rainbow sherbet 8%
Cookie dough 12%
Vanilla bean 26%

Total Number of Students = 650

1. How many students like vanilla bean most? _____

2. How many students like mint chip, cookie dough, and rocky road best?

_____

3. How many more students like fudge ripple than cookies 'n cream?

_____

4. How many fewer students like rainbow sherbet than vanilla bean?

_____

5. If 325 students liked fudge ripple, what percent would that be?

_____

6. How many students like rainbow sherbet, chocolate, and fudge ripple best?

_____

At the Races

Lan and Nicole are in the citywide marathon. The marathon consists of five legs. Each leg covers a different distance. Read the table about the race. Then answer the questions below. Round up to the next whole number as needed.

Leg	Distance in kilometers
1	150.5
2	68.7
3	40.5
4	145
5	222.3

1. What is the total distance of the entire race?

   _____

2. A kilometer is equal to 0.621 mile. How many total miles is the race?

   _____

3. Nicole completed the fourth leg of the race twice as fast as Lan. Lan finished the fourth leg in 16 hours. What was Nicole's average speed (in kilometers per hour)?

   _____

4. What is the average distance in kilometers of all the legs?

   _____

5. Lan finished the race in 28 hours. What was her average speed for the race (in miles per hour)?

   _____

Mighty Mountains

Read about the highest points above sea level on each continent.
Then answer the questions. Round up to the next whole number as needed.

- The highest point on Earth is on the border of China and Nepal, where Mt. Everest soars to a height of 29,028 feet.

- The highest peak in South America is Aconcagua in Argentina. It is 22,834 feet high.

- Alaska's Mt. McKinley is the highest point in North America. It is 20,230 feet high.

- The famous Mt. Kilimanjaro is in Africa's Tanzania. It reaches a height of 19,340 feet.

- Antarctica's highest peak soars up to 16,864 feet. This mountain is named Vinson Massif.

- Mt. Blanc is in the Alps between France and Italy. It peaks at 15,771 feet.

- Australia's highest peak, Kosciusko, reaches to a height of 7,310 feet.

1. What is the average height of all the mountains? _____

2. If it took a climber 14 hours to climb Mt. Blanc, how many feet per hour did he or she travel? _____

3. How many yards higher is the tallest mountain than the shortest mountain?

   _____

4. A meter is equal to 3.28 feet. How many meters high is Mt. Everest?

   _____

5. How many meters higher is Mt. McKinley than Vinson Massif?

   _____

What Order?

Jamie, Mia, Ellie, Noah, Min, Tham, and Miguel are waiting in line to give their book report presentations.

- Four people are standing between Mia and Jamie.

- Mia is looking ahead at Min, who is next up to read.

- Mia is in front of Noah.

- Miguel is between Tham and Noah.

- Ellie is between Tham and Jamie.

Write the student's names in order, from first in line to last in line.

1. _____

2. _____

3. _____

4. _____

5. _____

6. _____

7. _____

School Daze

Figure out how far each student lives from school. Then answer the questions.

Darryl lives 13.5 miles farther from school than Jordan. Jordan lives 3 miles from school. Kim lives 4.3 miles closer to school than Darryl. Sierra lives 2.5 times farther from school than Jordan. Jerome lives half as far from school as Kim.

1. How many miles from school does Kim live?

_____

2. How many miles from school does Sierra live?

_____

3. How many miles further from school does Darryl live than Jerome?

_____

4. How much further from school does the child with the furthest distance live than the child who lives the shortest distance?

_____

5. How many miles is Kim's roundtrip bus ride to and from school?

_____

6. Write the students' names in order, from closest to school to furthest.

_____

_____

_____

_____

_____

Train Trips

Read the train schedule below.

Then answer the questions.

Trains	A	B	C	D	E
Charlotte	7:15	8:10	9:05	10:38	12:20
Wilson	8:20	9:15	10:10	11:43	1:25
Daisy Falls	9:05	10:30	10:55	12:28	2:10
Redding	9:47	11:12	11:37	1:10	2:52
Ashton	11:28	12:23	1:18	2:51	4:33
Franklin	1:35	3:00	3:25	4:58	6:40
Storyville	2:55	4:20	4:45	6:18	8:00

1. How long does it take to get from Wilson to Ashton? _____

2. How long does it take to get from Daisy Falls to Storyville? _____

3. You took Train B from Wilson to Ashton. Then you picked up Train C to Franklin. How long did you spend on a train?

_____

4. You took Train D from Charlotte to Redding. Then you picked up Train E to Storyville. How long was your trip, from beginning to end?

_____

5. How long is it in Ashton between Train A and Train D?

_____

6. How long is it in Daisy Falls between Train B and Train E?

_____

7. You took Train B from Daisy Falls to Redding. Then you picked up Train D to Franklin. How long was your trip, from beginning to end?

_____

8. You took Train C to Redding. Then you picked up Train E to Storyville. How long was your wait between trains?

_____

Making Money

Read each problem carefully.

Then solve it.

1. Huma cleaned houses to save money for a new computer and printer. She cleaned three houses per week for two months at a rate of $25 per house. Then she increased her rate to $30 per house. She's been working at her new rate for three weeks. The computer and printer cost $1,320. How many more houses does Huma need to clean to buy the computer and printer?

   _____

2. There were 2,580 tickets sold in the school raffle. Of those tickets, 25% sold for $5.00 each, 30% sold for $2.75 each, and 40% sold for $4.50 each. The rest sold for $3.80 each. How much money did the raffle raise?

   _____

3. Mario delivers newspapers on Saturdays and Sundays. He makes $20 per day, with a 10% bonus each month. Mario has now worked six months. How much money has he made? _____

4. Mrs. Lorenzo's class raised $3,475 in the fundraiser. Of that money, 35% will be used for the school fair, 15% will be used to care for the class pet, and 20% will be used for field trips. The rest will be used for new art supplies. How much money will be used for each item?

   School fair: _____

   Class pet: _____

   Field trips: _____

   Art supplies: _____

Magic Squares

Fill in the missing numbers in the magic squares.

Here are the rules:
- You can't use a number more than once.
- All columns and rows must add up to the same number.

1. All columns and rows add up to 16.

2		10
	12	
		5

2. All columns and rows add up to 19.

	3	
7	11	
		14

3. All columns and rows add up to 23.

13	7	
2		
	6	

4. All columns and rows add up to 30.

10		15
	12	
		8

Extreme Weather

Read each problem carefully. Then solve it.

Round up to the next whole number as needed.

1. Several major snowstorms roared
   through the town of Winchester.
   One week, 22.5 inches of snow fell.
   The next week, 18.5 inches fell. The
   third week, 21.2 inches fell. The fourth
   week, 15.3 inches fell. The storms
   ended on week five, when another
   11.6 inches fell.

   How many inches of snow fell
   altogether? _____

   What was the average snowfall for the
   first three weeks? _____

   What was the median snowfall for the entire storm? _____

2. This winter was extremely cold! One day the temperature went from 52°F to −45°F! At
   noon, the temperature was 52°F. Over the next eight hours, the temperature dropped
   to 45°F, 37°F, 30°F, 21°F, 14°F, −12°F, −26°F, and finally −45°F.

   What was the mean temperature between noon and 5:00 PM? _____

   What was the median temperature between noon and 8:00 PM? _____

   What was the range in temperature between noon and 8:00 PM? _____

3. Winchester also got a lot of rain last year. It received the following rainfall
   measurements, in order, over six months: 10.2 in., 6.9 in., 12.7 in., 13.5 in., 18.6 in.,
   and 10.4 in.

   What was total rainfall over six months? _____

   What was the mean rainfall over six months? _____

   What was the range in rainfall over six months? _____

Tree Diagrams

Tanya is getting ready for her first day of school. She can wear a white, yellow, or pink blouse. She can choose black pants, khaki pants, jeans, or a denim skirt. How many different outfits does Tanya have?

Make tree diagrams to show your answers.

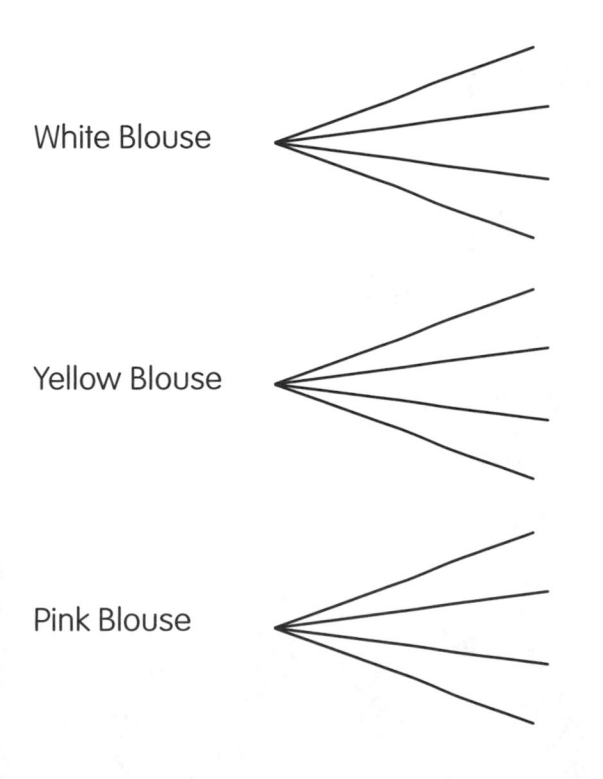

White Blouse

Yellow Blouse

Pink Blouse

How many total outfits does Tanya have to choose from? _____

Bank Account

Tarik just opened a bank account. Read all the deposits and debits listed below.

Then fill out the bankbook on the next page. The first entry has been done for you.

- On June 18, Tarik opened his bank account with $1,025.75.
- On June 30, he deposited a paycheck for $150.25.
- On July 3, he bought a new surfboard for $299.89.
- On July 12, he bought a wetsuit for $129.50.
- On July 15, he deposited a paycheck for $165.38.
- On July 17, he bought some new clothes for $47.95.
- On July 29, he bought his dad a new fishing pole for $89.42.
- On August 2, he deposited a paycheck for $95.77.
- On August 14, he deposited a birthday check for $50.00.
- On August 23, he donated $75.00 to the animal shelter.

Fill in the bankbook below.

Date	Description	Debit	Deposit	Balance
6/18	Opened bank account			1,025.75

1. What are Tarik's total debits? _____

2. What are Tarik's total deposits? _____

3. What is Tarik's ending balance as of August 23? _____

Making Measures

Help these amateur chefs figure out the measurements
they need by using this chart.

8 ounces (oz.) = 1 cup

16 ounces (oz.) = 1 pound

2 cups = 1 pint (pt.)

2 pints = 1 quart (qt.)

4 quarts = 1 gallon

3 teaspoons (tsp.) = 1 tablespoon (Tbs.)

1 liter = 1,000 milliliters (ml)

1 liter = about 4 cups

.50 liter = about 2 cups

1. Emily is making 16 gallons of fruit punch. She needs $2\frac{1}{3}$ cups of sugar for each gallon.

   How many cups of sugar does she need? _____

   How many pints of sugar does she need? _____

2. Armando is making chocolate chip cookies. For 2 dozen, he needs $3\frac{1}{4}$ teaspoons of vanilla.

   How many teaspoons does he need for 6 dozen? _____

   How many tablespoons does he need for 12 dozen? _____

3. Wyatt is using 4 liters of chicken broth in his chicken noodle soup. He's splitting the broth between two large pots on the stove.

How many milliliters of chicken broth go in each pot? _____

About how many cups go in each pot? _____

4. Jason is adding 1 quart more of water to his lemonade than Bailey. Bailey is adding $2\frac{1}{4}$ cups more than Sam. Sam is adding $3\frac{1}{2}$ cups.

How many cups of water is Jason adding to his lemonade?

_____

How many ounces of water is Bailey adding to his lemonade?

_____

5. Katie is tripling her super spicy chili recipe. She now needs 9 pounds of ground beef and 7 cups of kidney beans.

How many ounces of ground beef were needed for the original recipe?

_____

How many ounces of kidney beans does she need for the tripled recipe?

_____

If Katie only doubled her original recipe, how many pounds of ground beef would she need? _____

6. The apple crisp recipe calls for $2\frac{3}{4}$ teaspoons of cinnamon. Lauren is using 11 tablespoons.

How many teaspoons is she using? _____

How many apple crisps is she making? _____

Dinner Table

Kendra, Jackson, Brianna, Alex, Anna, and Danny each ordered a different dinner.
They ordered a steak, hamburger, pizza, chicken, cobb salad, and lasagna.
Use the clues to match each child with his or her dinner.

- Brianna's dinner came on a bun with fries.
- The name of Jackson's dinner begins with a "C."
- Danny doesn't eat red meat.
- Kendra's dinner is served cold.
- Anna's dinner came with three different toppings.

	Steak	Hamburger	Pizza	Chicken	Cobb Salad	Lasagna
Kendra						
Jackson						
Brianna						
Alex						
Anna						
Danny						

Shapes and Numbers

Read the clues to find the correct number.

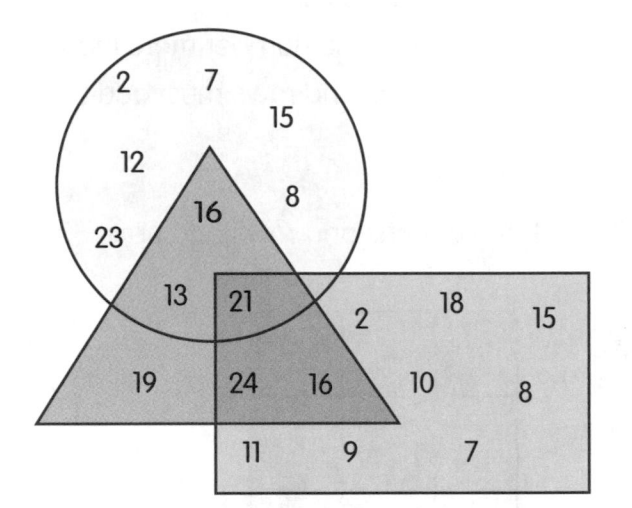

1. It is not an even number.
   It is in the rectangle and the triangle.
   It is more than 13.
   What is the number? _____

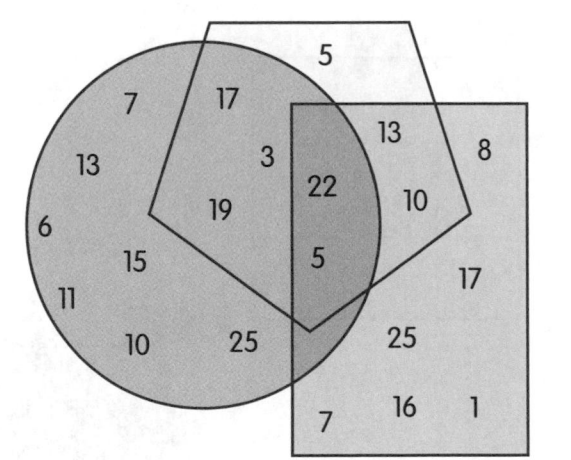

2. It is an even number.
   It is not in the pentagon.
   It is divisible by 3.
   What is the number? _____

More Magic Squares

Fill in the missing numbers in the magic squares.

Here are the rules:
- You can't use a number more than once.
- All columns and rows must add up to the same number.

1. All columns and rows add up to 33.

14		6
1		17

2. All columns and rows add up to 36.

18		
	12	
8		19

3. All columns and rows add up to 40.

22		
	17	
6	15	

4. All columns and rows add up to 45.

		10
	19	
16		18

Soccer Tournament

Read the problem carefully. Then answer the question.

Hint: It may help to draw a chart or make a list.

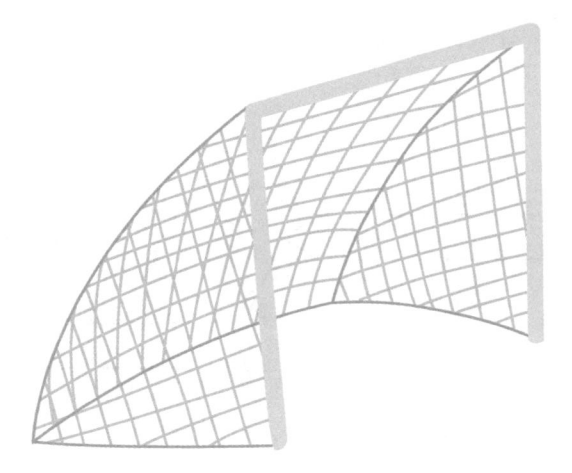 

Juvia's soccer team, the Comets, entered the all-state soccer tournament.

- In Round 1, all 40 teams played each of the other teams. The 30 teams who won the most games played in round 2.

- In Round 2, all 30 teams played each of the other teams. The 24 teams who won the most games played in round 3.

- In Round 3, all 24 teams played each of the other teams. The 10 teams who won the most games played in round 4.

- In Round 4, all 10 teams played each of the other teams. The 4 teams who won the most games played in the semifinals.

- In the semifinals, each of the 4 teams played one game. The winner of these two games played in the finals.

- The Comets played in the finals and won the game and the tournament.

How many total soccer games did the Comets play? _____

Basketball Math

Look at the team brackets for the basketball tournament.

Then answer the questions.

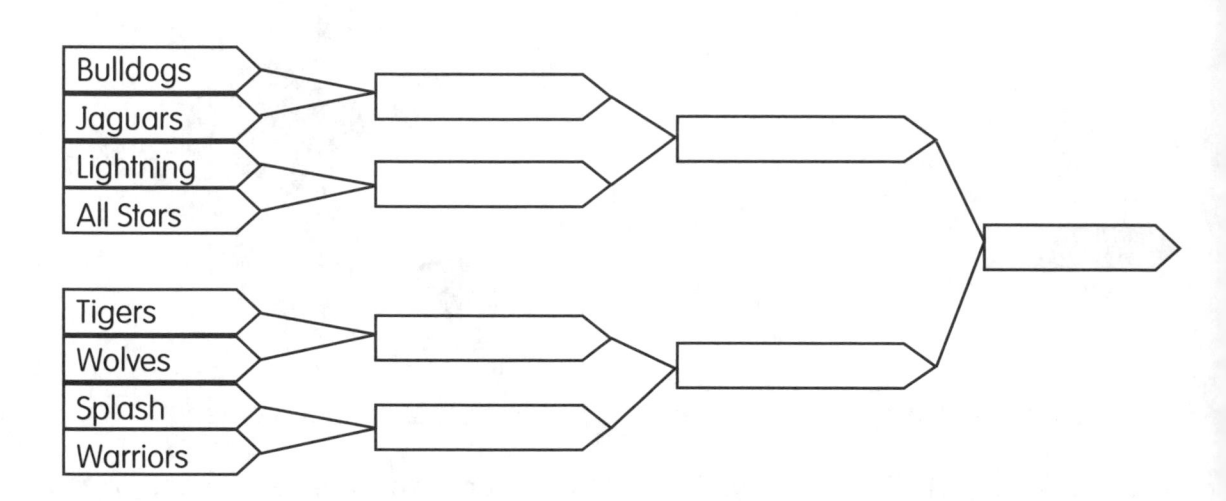

1. Each team had to win eight games to make it into the tournament. By the time a team wins the tournament, how many total games will it have to play and win?

   _____

2. In round 1, the Wolves scored 117 points to beat the Tigers by 11. The Splash beat the Warriors by 24 points. The final combined score of all four teams was 437 points. How many points did each team score?

   Wolves: _____

   Tigers: _____

   Splash: _____

   Warriors: _____

3. In round 1, the Jaguars scored 12 more points than the Lightning. The All Stars scored 18 more points than the Bulldogs. The Bulldogs scored 5 fewer points than the Lightning. The Lightning scored 113 points. How many points did each team score?

Jaguars: _____

Lightning: _____

All Stars: _____

Bulldogs: _____

4. Based on the scores in questions 2 and 3, which four teams went on to play in round 2? Fill in the team names in the brackets.

5. In round 2, the Jaguars scored 10 fewer points than the All Stars. The All Stars scored 16 more points than the Wolves. The Splash scored 8 fewer points than the Wolves. The Wolves scored 127 points. Who won each game? (Fill in the team numbers in the brackets.)

6. In the championship round, the All Stars scored 33 points in the 1st quarter and 19 points in the 2nd quarter. The Wolves scored 46 points in the 1st quarter and 12 points in the 2nd quarter. The All Stars scored 21 points in the 3rd quarter and 48 points in the 4th quarter. The Wolves scored 52 points in the 3rd quarter and 16 points in the 4th quarter. Who won the championship? Write the final scores below and write the winning team's name in the last bracket.

The All Stars: _____

The Wolves: _____

What's the Rule?

Can you guess the patterns? Write the rule for each pattern.
Then fill in the missing numbers.

1.

21	6
35	
17	2
	27
75	60
	41

Rule: _____

2.

1	2
2	4
3	6
	8
	12
	20

Rule: _____

3.

3	30
10	
12	39
	36
15	
	54

Rule: _____

4.

39	
75	25
99	33
	16
	22
135	

Rule: _____

For the Team

Coach Rhabar's softball team is selling discount movie tickets to save money for new team uniforms. Together, the team sold 424 tickets.

- Caprice sold $\frac{1}{4}$ of the tickets.
- Amanda sold 36 tickets less than Caprice.
- Maya sold 15 fewer tickets than Meena.
- Janelle sold $\frac{1}{4}$ as many tickets as Maya.
- Lisa sold 65 tickets more than Janelle.
- Meena sold half as many tickets as Amanda.
- The other girls on the team sold the rest of the tickets.

1. How many tickets did each girl sell?

Caprice: _____

Amanda: _____

Maya: _____

Janelle: _____

Lisa: _____

Meena: _____

2. Which two girls sold the same number of tickets? _____

_____

3. How many tickets did the rest of the team sell? _____

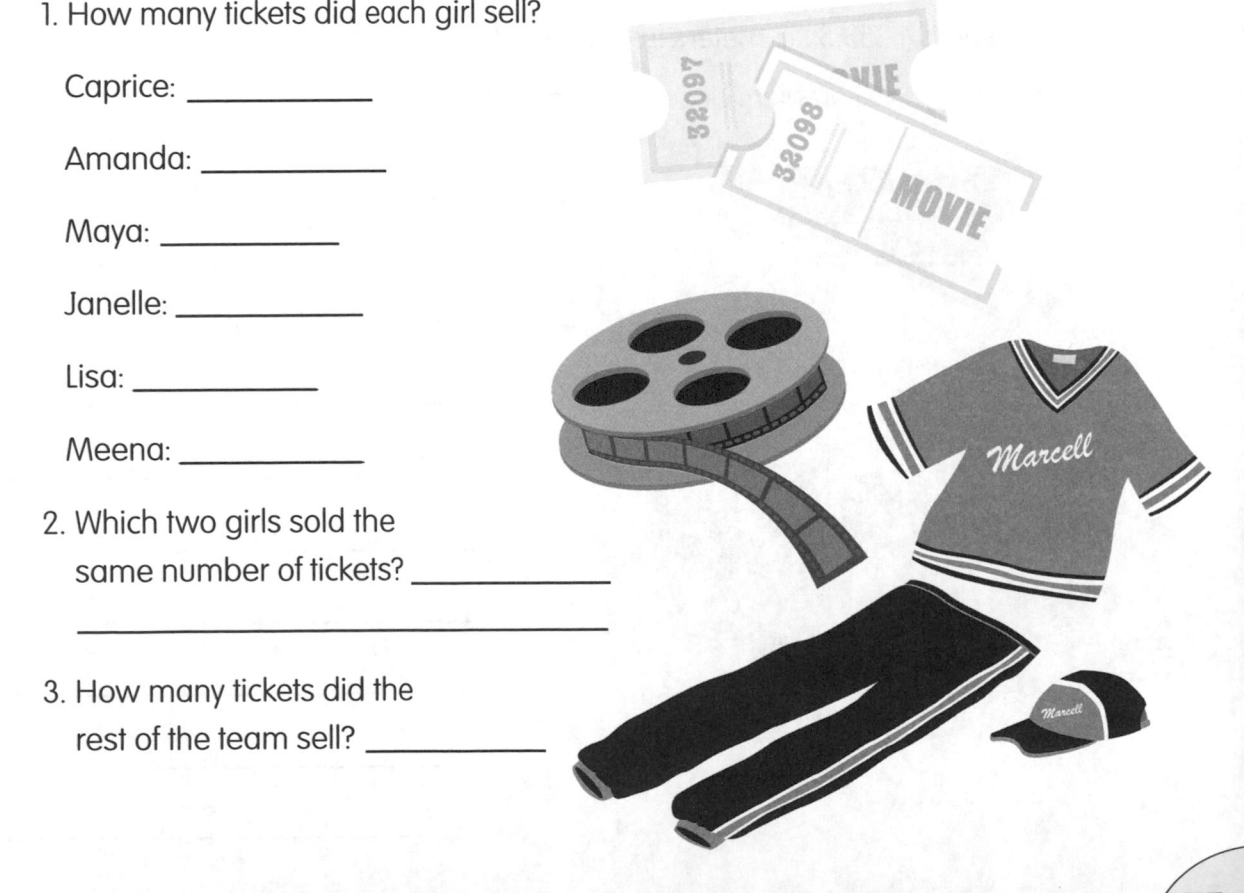

Figuring Distances

Read the problem and compare the distances. Then answer
the questions. Round up or down as needed.

Ahmed lives in Windy Shores. He travels often to the towns below, which are all
along the same road.

• Kilroy is 806.5 kilometers away from Windy Shores.

• Shasta is 540.9 kilometers further than Kilroy.

• Sunshine is 1,399.7 kilometers further than Shasta.

• Misty Mountain is 515.3 kilometers closer than Kilroy.

• Ferrington is 1,258.5 kilometers further than Misty Mountain.

• Carlyle is 748.4 kilometers closer than Ferrington.

WELCOME TO
SHASTA

1. Write the city names in order,
   from farthest to closest. Write the
   kilometers next to each city.

_____

_____

_____

_____

_____

_____

Road Rules

2. How many kilometers is it from Shasta to Sunshine? _____

3. How many kilometers is it from Misty Mountain to Ferrington? _____

4. A mile is equal to .621 kilometers. How far is it from Carlyle to Ferrington, in miles? (Round up or down if needed) _____

5. Ahmed drove from Windy Shores to Sunshine. Then he drove back to Kilroy. How many kilometers did he drive? _____

6. Ahmed drove halfway to Kilroy from Windy Shores before stopping for the night. The next day, he continued on to Sunshine in a plane. After stopping for another night, he took a plane back to Windy Shores. How many kilometers did he travel on the plane? _____

7. Ahmed took the train to Misty Mountain where he picked up his rental car. From there, he drove to Kilroy, and then on to Ferrington. After staying in Ferrington for a few days, he drove back to Carlyle where he dropped off his rental car. He took the train back home to Windy Shores. How many kilometers did Ahmed drive?

_____

Reading Contest

Ms. Chang's sixth grade class had a reading contest. The three groups competed to see who could read the most pages. Ms. Chang created a chart of the number of pages each group read.

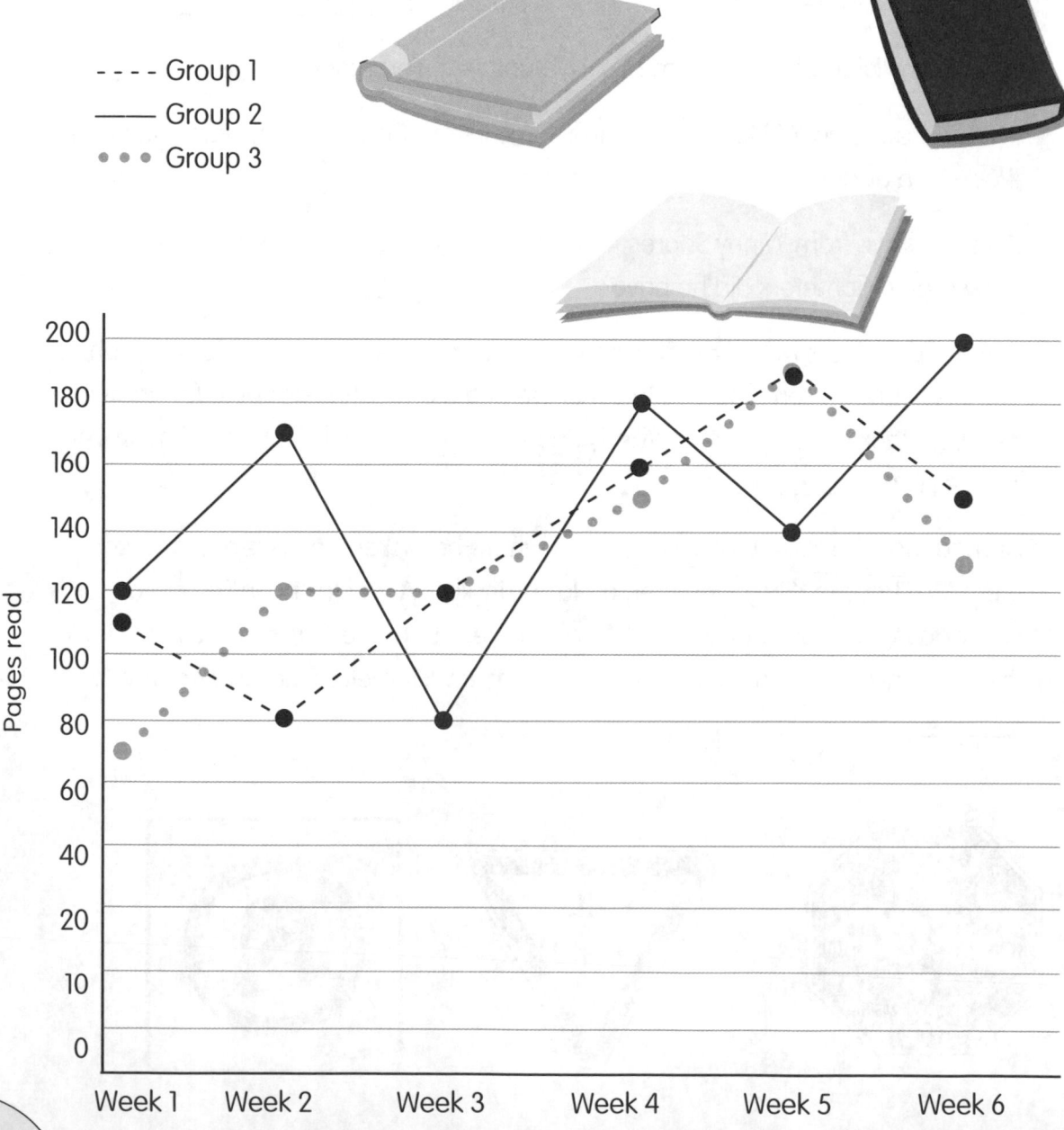

- - - - Group 1
——— Group 2
• • • Group 3

1. Who read the most pages, Group 1, 2, or 3? _____

2. How many pages did all groups read in Week 1? _____

3. How many pages did all groups read in Week 3? _____

4. In what week were the fewest number of pages read? _____
   How many fewer pages were read in this week than the week with
   the most pages read? _____

5. How many total pages did the groups read in six weeks?

   _____

6. If each book had 26 pages, about how many books were read?

   _____

7. What was the average number of pages read each week over six weeks?
   (Round up or down if needed.) _____

Favorite Sports

Gia and her friends all play different sports. Read the clues to find out who plays each sport. Write the names and sports on the lines around the soccer ball.

The children are:

Gia
Nick
Anh
Mario

The sports are:

soccer
ice hockey
tennis
baseball

Clues:

1. A boy whose name begins with "N" plays a winter sport. He is sitting across from Anh.

2. Gia is not sitting next to the boy who enjoys soccer.

3. Anh does not play tennis or ice hockey.

_____

_____

_____ Anh

_____

_____

_____ soccer

On the Blueprint

The Moreno family is building a new house.
Look at the measurements on the blueprint below.

12 ft.	12 ft. Bathroom	20 ft. Bedroom #1
25 ft.	Living Room	
15 ft.	Kitchen	Dining Room
10 ft.	Utility Room	Bedroom #2
20 ft.	Garage	
	28 ft.	

1. The master bedroom is usually bigger than other bedrooms in a house. Which bedroom would be considered the master bedroom?

_____

2. What is the area of both bedrooms put together?

_____

3. What is larger, the combined perimeter around the kitchen and utility room or the perimeter of the garage?

_____

4. What is smaller, the combined area of the dining room and bedroom #2 or the combined area of the living room?

_____

5. What is the perimeter and area of the whole house and garage?

Perimeter: _____

Area: _____

Time for School

Mr. Gonzales is buying school supplies for all six of his children. He made a special list for each child, but then he mixed up the lists. Use the clues below to help Mr. Gonzales match the correct list with each child. He used a $20 bill to pay for each child's supplies.

Item	Price
calculator	$3.35
box of pencils	$1.25
notebook	75¢
highlighter	98¢
box of pens	$2.49
stapler	$2.99
pencil sharpener	$1.05
erasers	59¢
binder	$1.50

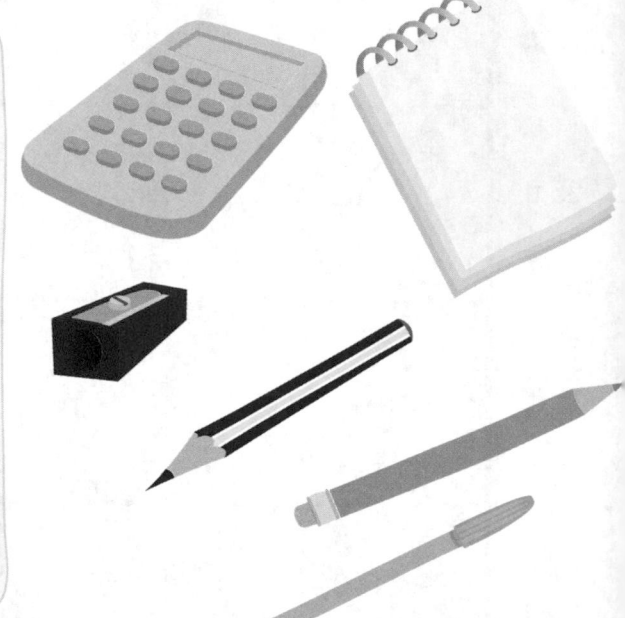

- Alana needs one of everything, except a pencil sharpener. Mr. Gonzales got $6.10 in change.

- Kevin is getting the same number of erasers as Hector, but more pencils.

- Evelina only needs writing supplies. Mr. Gonzales got 41¢ in change.

- Manny is getting the same number of each item. Mr. Gonzales got $4.72 in change.

- When Mr. Gonzales bought Nora's supplies, he got $1.72 in change.

Time for School

List 1 _____

1 pencil sharpener

3 highlighters

6 erasers

2 binders

1 calculator

1 box of pencils

List 2 _____

4 boxes of pencils

1 calculator

1 stapler

2 boxes of pens

2 highlighters

List 3 _____

6 erasers

2 boxes of pencils

4 notebooks

2 binders

1 stapler

List 4 _____

1 calculator

1 box of pencils

1 notebook

1 highlighter

1 box of pens

1 stapler

1 eraser

1 binder

List 5 _____

4 binders

4 erasers

4 highlighters

4 notebooks

List 6 _____

4 boxes of pens

3 box of pencils

6 highlighters

1. Write the name of each child on his or her list.

2. How much more did the most expensive list of supplies cost than the least
   expensive? _____

3. How much did the children's supplies cost altogether? _____

4. After paying for all the supplies, how much money did Mr. Gonzales have leftover?

   _____

On Sale!

Jenna and Naoki went to the mall for the big fall sale. Read each problem to figure out how much they spent. Round up or down as needed.

$ 36.99

1. Naoki got his tennis shoes on sale at 20% off. But he also had a coupon for an additional 10% off of the sale price. How much did he spend?

_____

2. Jenna bought three pairs of jeans. Then she decided to go back and get another pair for her twin sister, Jill. How much did she spend for all four pairs?

_____

$ 25.50
BUY 2
GET 1 50% OFF!

$10.00

3. Naoki had coupons for 15% off of three video games. He used two coupons to buy six video games. How much did he spend?

_____

4. Jenna needed a new tennis racquet for her school tennis team. She bought one racquet and two cans of tennis balls for $3.99 each. How much did she spend? _____

$ 42.95
All Tennis Equipment
33 % OFF!

5. Naoki needed a new chalk and paint set for his art class. Luckily he cut out a coupon for $5.00 off the sale price. How much did he spend? _____

6. Jenna spotted a special deal: "Buy a coat and get the scarf and mittens $\frac{1}{3}$ off." She decided to buy them all. If she gave the cashier four $20 bills, how much change did she receive?

_____

7. Naoki and Jenna stopped for lunch in the food court. They each ordered a sandwich and a drink. The price of each sandwich was $3.50. The drinks were $1.15 each. The tax was 4.25%. If Jenna gave the cashier $10.00, how much change did she receive?

_____

8. Naoki bought his mom new earrings and flowers for her birthday. He had a 15% off coupon for the flowers, and the earrings were on sale for $\frac{1}{4}$ off. How much did Naoki spend on his mom's birthday presents?

_____

Baseball Cards

Read the information on the back of this baseball card.

Then answer the questions.

Brady Chance
3rd Base, Baltimore Thunder

Brady Chance plays third base for the Baltimore Thunder. He has been playing with this team for six years.

Year	BA	H	HR	SO	BB	G	AB
1999	.302	114	27	45	19	140	460
2000	.287	110	37	70	20	140	502
2001	.334	124	18	62	13	145	422
2002	.231	90	24	104	16	144	476
2003	.189	108	28	98	11	141	419
2004	.290	68	26	76	21	145	442

BA = Batting Average
H = Hits
HR = Home runs
SO = Strikeouts
BB = Walks (bases on balls)
G = Games
AB = At Bats (number of times at bat)

1. In what year did Chance get the most home runs?

_____

2. How many more times did he strike out in 2002 than in 1999?

_____

3. A batting average higher than .275 is considered good. Based on Chances' play over these six years, would you say he's a good player?

_____

4. How many times was Chance at bat in 2002–2004?

_____

5. In which year did Chance have the best batting average?

_____

In which year did he have the worst batting average?

_____

What is the difference between the two?

_____

6. If Chance hit a grand slam for 5% of the home runs he's hit in these six years, how many runs would he score from grand slams? (Hint: A grand slam scores four runs.)

_____

7. If Chance scored 25% of the times he walked, how many runs would he score?

_____

Perimeter, Area, and Volume

Read the problems and answer the questions below.

Round up or down to the nearest whole number.

1. Josh is building small wading pools for his neighbors. The Jones' pool is 9.3 feet long by 6.5 feet wide by 3 feet deep. The Webbs' pool is 8.9 feet long by 6.4 feet wide by 2.5 feet deep. The Grangers' pool is 10.2 feet long by 5 feet wide by 2.8 feet deep. Whose pool holds the most cubic feet of water? _____

   What is the difference in volume between the largest pool and the smallest pool?

   _____

   List the pools in order, from smallest perimeter to largest perimeter:

   _____   _____   _____

2. Lei planted three gardens in her backyard. The rose tgarden is 13.2 feet x 18.7 feet. The tomato garden is 10.3 feet x 20 feet. The sunflower garden is 15.5 feet x 17.5 feet. Which garden has the largest area? _____

   What is it? _____ sq. ft.

   What is the difference in area between the largest garden and the smallest garden? _____ sq. ft.

   What is the total area of all three gardens? _____ sq. ft.

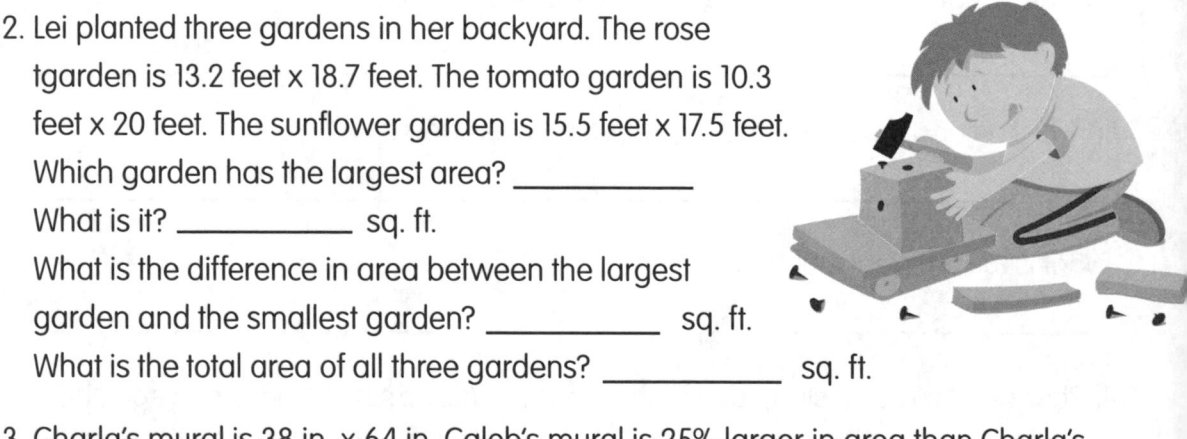

3. Charla's mural is 38 in. x 64 in. Caleb's mural is 25% larger in area than Charla's. Tao's mural is half the area as that of Caleb's. Summer's mural is 35% larger in area than Tao's. List the area of each child's mural in order, from smallest to largest:

   Name   Area

   _____   _____

   _____   _____

   _____   _____

   _____   _____

Jorge's Babysitting Service

Jorge runs a babysitting service for his friends. Based on his or her experience, each person charges a different rate per hour. Look at the list and then answer the questions. Round up or down as needed.

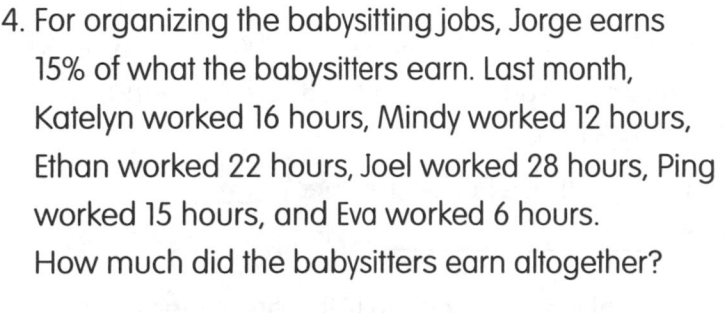

Babysitting Charges, Per Hour

Katelyn	$4.35
Mindy	$4.75
Ethan	$3.00
Joel	$4.50
Ping	$2.75
Eva	$3.75

1. Jorge wants to raise the rate of all the babysitters by 20%. How much will each person charge then?

   Katelyn: _____   Joel: _____

   Mindy: _____   Ping: _____

   Ethan: _____   Eva: _____

2. What is the average rate originally charged by the babysitters? _____

3. Jorge's friend Kayla wants to join the babysitting service. She wants her rate to be exactly in between the highest and lowest rate. How much should she charge per hour? _____

4. For organizing the babysitting jobs, Jorge earns 15% of what the babysitters earn. Last month, Katelyn worked 16 hours, Mindy worked 12 hours, Ethan worked 22 hours, Joel worked 28 hours, Ping worked 15 hours, and Eva worked 6 hours. How much did the babysitters earn altogether?

   _____

   How much did Jorge earn? _____

In the Ocean

Read the following information about oceans.

Then answer the questions. Round up or down as needed.

Ocean	Average depth	Deepest point
Pacific	13,740 feet	Mariana Trench: 38,635 feet
Atlantic	12,254 feet	Puerto Rico Trench: 30,184 feet
Indian	12,740 feet	Java Trench: 24,344 feet
Arctic	3,407 feet	Eurasia Basin: 17,881 feet

1. What is the average depth of the ocean floor? _____

2. How much deeper is the Mariana Trench than the Eurasia Basin?

    _____

3. The highest point on Earth above sea level is Mt. Everest. It peaks at 29,028 feet. The deepest point on Earth is the Mariana Trench. What is the total number of feet between these high and low points? _____

4. There are many other deep trenches in the Pacific Ocean, including: Tonga Trench (35,505 ft.), Japan Trench (34,626 ft.), Kurile Trench (34,587 ft.), Mindanao Trench (34,439 ft.), and Kermadec Trench (32,963).
   What is the average depth of all of these Pacific trenches? _____
   What is the range in depth? _____

5. One of the greatest creatures that live in the ocean is the great white shark. A shark will "shed" and replace about 30,000 of its teeth in its lifetime. If a shark lives to be 25 years old, about how many teeth per year will it shed?

    _____

Amazing Maze

Solve each problem. Then use each answer to find your way through the maze.

1. $195 \div (3 \times 5) + 3^3$
2. $(5^5 \div 25) + 15$
3. $248 + (35 \times 19)$
4. $2^3 + 8^3 + 4^4$
5. $3^4 + 16 - (9 \times 5)$

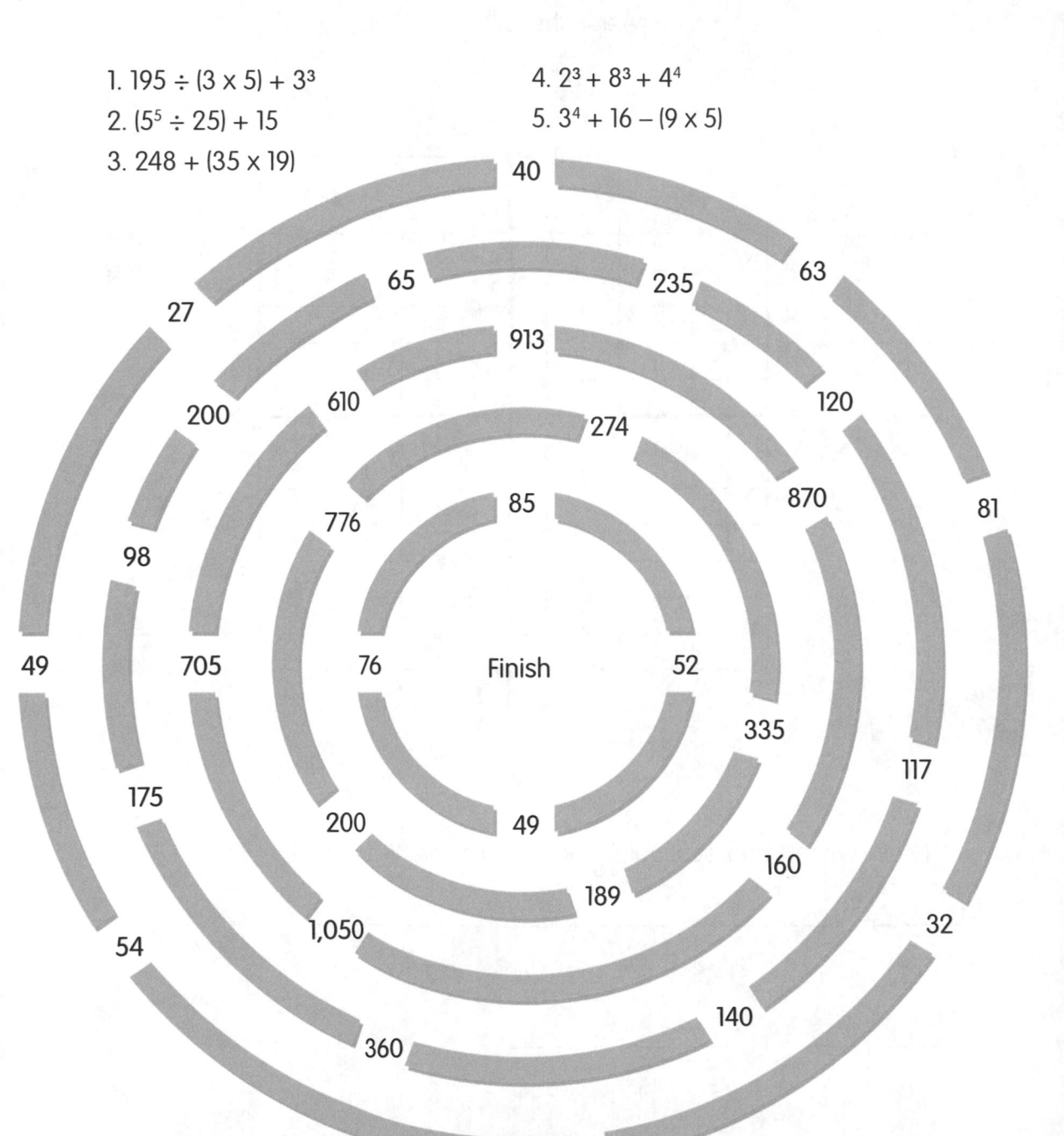

Crack the Code

Use the letters in the graph to find the
answer to the following riddles.

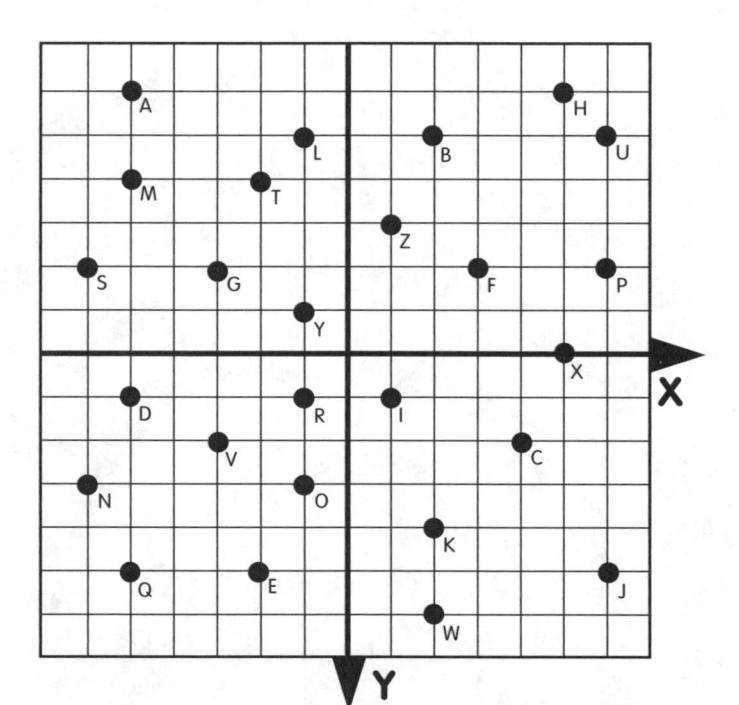

1. I have wheels and flies, but I'm not an airplane. What am I?

_____ _____ _____ _____ _____ _____ _____

-3,2   -5,6   -1,-1   2,5   -5,6   -3,2   -2,-5

_____ _____ _____ _____ _____

-2,4   -1,-1   6,5   4,-2   2,-4

2. I can sizzle like bacon, but I am made with an egg. I do have a backbone, but lack good legs. I can peel like an onion, but I still remain whole. I am long like a flagpole, yet I fit in a hole. What am I?

___ ___ ___ ___ ___
-6,2   -6,-3   -5,6   2,-4   -2,-5

3. On the Earth as we know it, a day follows a day. But there is a place where yesterday always follows today. What place is that?

___ ___ ___ ___ ___ ___ ___ ___ ___ ___
-5,-1   1,-1   4,-2   -2,4   1,-1   -1,-3   -6,-3   -5,6   -1,-1   -1,1

4. What word has more letters in it than any other?

___ ___ ___ ___ ___ ___ ___ ___
-5,6   -1,5   6,2   5,6   -5,6   2,5   -2,-5   -2,4

5. What do you call an angry wild pig?

___ ___ ___ ___   ___ ___ ___ ___
-6,2   -1,-3   -1,-1   -2,-5   2,5   -1,-3   -5,6   -1,-1

Answer Key

Page 4
1. 330°F 2. 264.6°F
3. 100°; Browning 4. −21°F

Page 5
1. 58.2 pounds 2. $4\frac{7}{12}$ feet
3. $3\frac{1}{15}$ feet 4. 181.7 pounds
5. $4\frac{1}{6}$ feet

Pages 6–7
1. 11:52 PM
2. 1:10 PM; 6:27 PM
3. 7:05 PM; 10:18 PM
4. 5:02 PM; 6:54 PM

Page 8
$162 = 6 \times (12 + 15)$
$(30 \times 2) - 12 = 48$
$(156 \div 12) + 70 = 83$
$232 = (8 \times 37) - 64$
$(93 - 27) \div 11 = 6$
$45 + (80 \times 12) = 1,005$

Page 9
1. a. $\frac{12}{69}$ b. $\frac{30}{69}$ c. $\frac{27}{69}$
2. a. $\frac{4}{7}$ b. $\frac{1}{7}$ c. $\frac{2}{7}$
3. a. $\frac{38}{73}$ b. $\frac{10}{73}$ c. $\frac{56}{73}$

Page 10
1. $2,268 2. buy
3. $31,524 4. lease
5. $17,090.75

Page 11
1. Diameter: 27 inches
   Circumference: 85 inches
2. Diameter: 36 inches (1 yard)
   Circumference: 113 inches
   (3 yards)
3. Diameter: 24 inches
   Circumference: 75 inches
4. Diameter: 11 inches
   Circumference: 35 inches

Page 12
1. 45 degrees; right triangle
2. 73 degrees; acute triangle
3. 60 degrees; equilateral
   triangle
4. 18 degrees; obtuse triangle
5. 60 degrees; equilateral
   triangle

Page 13
1. roast turkey sandwich
   with cheese and pasta
   salad
2. $34.30
3. $1.75; $1.60
4. Caesar salad, vegetarian
   sandwich with cheese,
   and one bag of chips

Pages 14–15
1. Blue Cave Beach
2. Ocean Mist Beach
3. Shell Beach
4. 900,000
5. 600,001
6. 7,950,000
7. Ocean Mist Beach: 750,000
   Dolphin Beach: 1,050,000
   Shell Beach: 1,200,000
   Pismo Beach: 1,500,000
   Moonstone Beach: 1,650,000
   Blue Cave Beach: 1,800,000

Pages 16–17
1. Rent: $5,000
   Utilities: $2,000
   Clothing: $2,500
   Food: $3,000
   Car: $2,250
   Medical: $1,000
   Taxes: $2,500
   Savings: $1,250
   Entertainment: $2,000
   Miscellaneous: $3,500
2. no; $33
3. $500; yes
4. $1,125; $4,625
5. $1,940
6. $625

Page 18
Pepperoni: onions, ham,
olives, mushrooms, sausage,
pineapple, peppers
Onions: ham, olives,
mushrooms, sausage,
pineapple, peppers
Ham: olives, mushrooms,
sausage, pineapple, peppers
Olives: mushrooms, sausage,
pineapple, peppers
Mushrooms: sausage,
pineapple, peppers
Sausage: pineapple,
peppers
Pineapple: peppers

Page 19
Chocolate Chip Cookies

Ingredient	1 dozen	12 dozen	15 dozen
shortening	1 cup	12 cups	15 cups
sugar	$1\frac{2}{3}$ cups	20 cups	25 cups
eggs	2	24	30
flour	$4\frac{1}{4}$ cups	51 cups	$63\frac{3}{4}$ cups
vanilla	$1\frac{1}{2}$ tsp.	18 tsp.	$22\frac{1}{2}$ tsp.
baking soda	$\frac{3}{4}$ tsp.	9 tsp.	$11\frac{1}{4}$ tsp.
chocolate chips	$1\frac{1}{3}$ cups	16 cups	20 cups

Spaghetti with Marina Sauce

Ingredient	1 recipe	6 recipes	13 recipes
tomatoes	3 pounds	18 pounds	39 pounds
chicken stock	$5\frac{1}{2}$ cups	33 cups	$71\frac{1}{2}$ cups
garlic	4 cloves	24 cloves	52 cloves
basil	$1\frac{1}{4}$ tsp.	$7\frac{1}{2}$ tsp.	$16\frac{1}{2}$ tsp.
oregano	2 tsp.	12 tsp.	26 tsp.
spaghetti	1 pound	6 pounds	13 pounds

Page 20
1. 6,000 cubic feet
2. Box A; 6 cubic feet
3. 30 cubic feet
4. 7,776 cubic inches; 260 bags

Page 21
1. 169 2. 202
3. 72 4. 117
5. 50% 6. 234

Page 22
1. 627 kilometers
2. 389 miles
3. 18 kilometers per hour
4. 104.5 kilometers
5. 14 miles per hour

Page 23
1. 18,768 feet 2. 1,127 feet
3. 7,239 yards 4. 8,850 meters
5. 1,026 meters

Page 24
1. Min; 2. Mia; 3. Noah; 4. Miguel;
5. Tham; 6. Ellie; 7. Jamie

Page 25
1. 12.2 miles 2. 7.5 miles
3. 10.4 miles 4. 13.5 miles
5. 24.4 miles
6. Jordan, Jerome, Sierra, Kim,
   Darryl

Pages 26–27
1. 3 hours, 8 minutes
2. 5 hours, 50 minutes
3. 5 hours, 15 minutes
4. 9 hours, 22 minutes
5. 3 hours, 23 minutes
6. 3 hours, 40 minutes
7. 6 hours, 28 minutes
8. 3 hours, 15 minutes

Page 28
1. 15 houses
2. $10,487.70
3. $1,056
4. School fair: $1,216.25
   Class pet: $521.25
   Field trips: $695.00
   Art supplies: $1,042.50

Page 29
1.
2	4	10
3	12	1
11	0	5

2.
12	3	4
7	11	1
0	5	14

3.
13	7	3
2	10	11
8	6	9

4.
10	5	15
11	12	7
9	13	8

Page 30
1. 89 inches; 21 inches;
   18.5 inches
2. 33°F; 21°F; 97°F
3. 72.3 in.; 12 in.; 11.7 in.

Page 31
White blouse — black pants, khaki pants, jeans, denim skirt
Yellow blouse — black pants, khaki pants, jeans, denim skirt
Pink blouse — black pants, khaki pants, jeans, denim skirt
Tanya has 12 total outfits.

Pages 32–33

Date	Description	Debit	Deposit	Balance
6/18	Open bank account			1,025
6/30	Deposit paycheck		150.25	1,176.
7/3	Surfboard	299.89		876.1
7/12	Wetsuit	129.50		746.6
7/15	Deposit paycheck		165.38	911.99
7/17	Clothes	47.95		864.0
7/29	Fishing pole	89.42		774.6
8/2	Deposit paycheck		95.77	870.3
8/14	Deposit birthday check		50.00	920.3
8/23	Animal shelter donation	75.00		845.3

1. $641.76
2. $1,487.15
3. $845.39

Answer Key

Pages 34–35
1. $37\frac{1}{3}$ cups; $18\frac{2}{3}$ pints
2. $9\frac{3}{4}$ teaspoons; $6\frac{1}{2}$ tablespoons
3. 2,000 milliliters; 8 cups
4. $9\frac{3}{4}$ cups; 46 ounces
5. 48 ounces; 56 ounces; 6 pounds
6. 33 teaspoons; 12 apple crisps

Page 36
Kendra: cobb salad
Jackson: chicken
Brianna: hamburger
Alex: steak
Anna: pizza
Danny: lasagna

Page 37
1. 21   2. 6

Page 38
1.
14	13	6
18	5	10
1	15	17

2.
18	15	3
10	12	14
8	9	19

3.
22	8	10
12	17	11
6	15	19

4.
20	15	10
9	19	17
16	11	18

Page 39
102 games

Pages 40–41
1. 11 games
2. Wolves: 117; Tigers: 106; Splash: 119; Warriors: 95
3. Jaguars: 125; Lightning: 113; All Stars: 126; Bulldogs: 108
4. The Jaguars played the All Stars; the Wolves played the Splash.
5. The All Stars and the Wolves
6. The All Stars: 121;
   The Wolves: 126
   The Wolves won the championship.

Page 42
1.
21	6
35	20
17	2
42	27
75	60
56	41

Rule: −15

2.
1	2
2	4
3	6
4	8
6	12
10	20

Rule: ×2

3.
3	30
10	37
12	39
9	36
15	42
27	54

Rule: +27

4.
39	13
75	25
99	33
48	16
66	22
135	45

Rule: ÷3

Page 43
1. Caprice: 106
   Amanda: 70
   Maya: 20
   Janelle: 5
   Lisa: 70
   Meena: 35
2. Amanda and Lisa
3. 118 tickets

Pages 44–45
1. Sunshine 2,747.1
   Ferrington 1,549.7
   Shasta 1,347.4
   Kilroy 806.5
   Carlyle 801.3
   Misty Mountain 291.2
2. 1,399.7 kilometers
3. 1,258.5 kilometers
4. 464.8 miles
5. 4,687.7 kilometers
6. 5,090.95 kilometers
7. 2,006.9 kilometers

Pages 46–47
1. Group 2
2. 300 pages
3. 320 pages
4. Week 1; 220
5. 2,480 pages
6. 95 books
7. 413 pages

Page 48
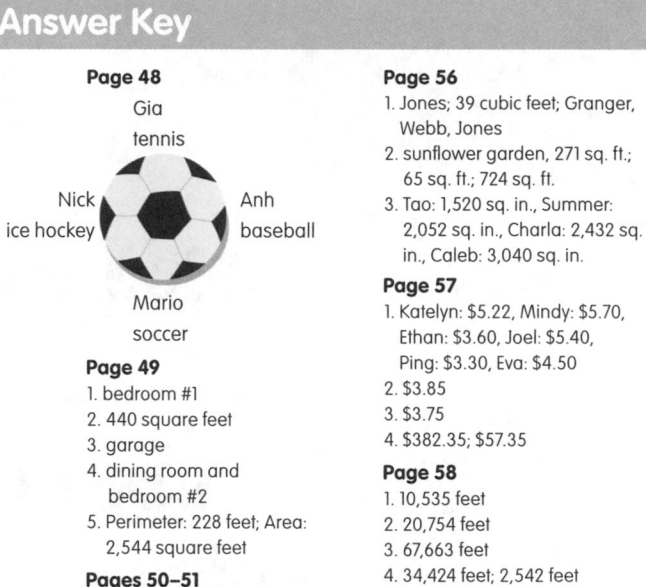

Gia
tennis

Nick
ice hockey

Anh
baseball

Mario
soccer

Page 49
1. bedroom #1
2. 440 square feet
3. garage
4. dining room and bedroom #2
5. Perimeter: 228 feet; Area: 2,544 square feet

Pages 50–51
1. List 1: Hector
   List 2: Nora
   List 3: Kevin
   List 4: Alana
   List 5: Manny
   List 6: Evelina
2. $5.69
3. $97.21
4. $22.79

Pages 52–53
1. $26.63
2. $89.25
3. $51.00
4. $34.12
5. $10.08
6. $17.05
7. 30¢
8. $20.24

Pages 54–55
1. 2000
2. 59
3. yes
4. 1,337
5. 2001; 2003; .145
6. 32 runs
7. 25 runs

Page 56
1. Jones; 39 cubic feet; Granger, Webb, Jones
2. sunflower garden, 271 sq. ft.; 65 sq. ft.; 724 sq. ft.
3. Tao: 1,520 sq. in., Summer: 2,052 sq. in., Charla: 2,432 sq. in., Caleb: 3,040 sq. in.

Page 57
1. Katelyn: $5.22, Mindy: $5.70, Ethan: $3.60, Joel: $5.40, Ping: $3.30, Eva: $4.50
2. $3.85
3. $3.75
4. $382.35; $57.35

Page 58
1. 10,535 feet
2. 20,754 feet
3. 67,663 feet
4. 34,424 feet; 2,542 feet
5. 1,200 teeth per year

Page 59

Pages 60–61
1. garbage truck
2. snake
3. dictionary
4. alphabet
5. sore boar

Nice work!

_____,
(Name)

you're a
problem solving
champion!